TANKS
in detail
Ausf A, D & G
PANZER V PANTHER

TANKS
in detail

Ausf A, D & G
PANZER V PANTHER

JONATHAN FORTY

Ian Allan
PUBLISHING

Acknowledgements

This book could not have been produced without
the invaluable assistance of the following people:
David Fletcher, Librarian at the Tank Museum *(TM)*,
Bovington, Dorset, England, and his staff; Roland Groom
(RG/TM), for original images and prints from archive
material; Bob Fleming *(RJF)* for the colour photographs
of the Panzer Museum's restored Panther; Hilary
Doyle/Panzer Tracts PO. Box 334, Boyds, ML20841
USA for the supply and use of the superb four-view line
drawings and finally to George Forty *(GF)* for access to his
vast knowledge and archive.

Jasper Spencer-Smith
Bournemouth, England
January 2003

Conceived & Edited by Jasper Spencer-Smith.
Executive Editor: George Forty.
Design and Illustration: Nigel Pell.
Produced by JSS Publishing Limited,
Bournemouth, Dorset, England.

First published 2003

ISBN 0 7110 2941 5

Published by Ian Allan Publishing

an imprint of Ian Allan Publishing Ltd, Hersham,
Surrey KT12 4RG.

Printed by Ian Allan Printing Ltd, Hersham,
Surrey KT12 4RG.

Code: 0304/A3

CONTENTS

CHAPTER ONE

DESIGN & DEVELOPMENT

During Operation Barbarossa, German armour was virtually invincible until the appearance on the battlefield of the Soviet's T-34. In response to this new threat the *Heereswaffenamt* hastened the development of a new heavily armoured and armed medium tank. The Panther Ausf D entered service at Kursk, July 1943.

Without doubt one of the biggest shocks the German *Panzertruppen* ever received during World War Two was their first encounter with Soviet T-34 tanks, in October 1941 in the Mzensk area of Russia, where they suffered severe losses. Up until this time the Germans had always considered their armoured fighting vehicles (AFVs) to be far superior to anything anyone else could produce, but with the advent of the T-34 clearly the situation had been reversed. Perhaps if they not been quite so smug about their apparent superiority the reversal might never have occurred. This was evidently the view of *Generaloberst* (Colonel General) Heinz Guderian, the prime instigator and guru of German AFV development and tactics, for in his autobiography he discussed a visit made by a Soviet delegation at Hitler's invitation in the spring of 1941, only a few months before the German invasion of the USSR, to look at Panzer training schools and tank-building factories. He recalled how insistent the visitors had been that they were not being shown the latest developments, despite reassurances to the contrary. They could not believe that the PzKpfw IV was the heaviest type of tank in German service and their scepticism led some people, including Guderian

himself, to conclude that perhaps the Soviet were already working on something bigger.

As the initial German assault of Operatio Barbarossa swept forward with ease throug Soviet armour a few months later these fear faded, only to be painfully reawakened whe the T-34 was then encountered in combat Guderian promptly advocated that a tean be sent out at once to make an on-the spot examination and formulate a response This team, composed of experts from th *Heereswaffenamt WaPrüf VI* (Army Ordnanc Office 6) and Armaments Ministry along wit tank designers and manufacturers, arrived at th 2nd Panzer Army front in November 1941 There they examined captured and knocke out T-34s and talked with the soldiers who ha come up against them - many of whom wer clearly of the opinion that the simplest an swiftest answer would be to replicate th T-34 exactly. However, due to the practica problems raised by this proposal the designer did not agree; it would have been impossible t mass-produce certain essential T-34 component such as its aluminium diesel engine, whil shortages of raw materials from which t manufacture steel alloys were an insurmountabl problem for Germany, suffering the effects of a

Above:
Awaiting repair and modification at the MHN factory in Hannover is this PanzerKampfwagen V Panther Ausf D. Note the distinctive letterbox-type MG slot and the driver's vision hatch in the glacis. The tank is fitted with two head-lamps, both without blackout covers. *(TM)*

Left:
Equipment boxes, one on each side, fitted to the rear hull plate. All Panthers from Ausf A were fitted with these boxes. Note the spare track links and towing equipment on the side of the tank. *(TM)*

Allied embargo. It was therefore decided to adopt a compromise solution, with the construction of a new medium tank based on the T-34 weighing around 35 tons (35,561.46kg), to be called Panther. So began the development of what many experts consider to be the best tank built by any nation during World War Two.

On 25 November 1941 the *Heereswaffenamt* issued contracts to Daimler-Benz and MAN (Maschinenfabrik Ausgburg-Nürnberg), to produce designs for the new tank as quickly as possible. It was given the designation VK

(*Volketten Kraftfahrzeug* – fully-tracked vehicle) 3002 and was to have the following specifications: weight: 30–35 tons (30,000–35,500kg) armour thickness (minimum): frontal arc 2.34in (60mm); sides and rear: 1.58in (40mm) – with both the front glacis and side armour to be sloped like that of the T-34; speed: 35mph (55km/h) maximum and 25mph (40km/h cruising and with a crew of five: driver, radio operator/hull gunner, commander, main gunner and loader. The two companies produced very different design proposals. The Daimler-Benz VK 3002(DB) closely resembled the T-34

while the MAN design, VK 3002(MAN), was closer to contemporary German tank designs. Essential differences between the two models were that the Daimler-Benz model weighed 34 tons (34,545.41kg), had a hull shape very similar to that of the T-34, a Daimler-Benz MB 507 diesel engine with a Maybach Olvar eight-speed gearbox and the main drive leading to rear-mounted sprockets, paired steel bogies suspended by leaf springs, the driver located within the turret cage and the main armament was a 7.5cm StuK (*SturmKanone*) L/48 gun.

The MAN model was 35 tons (35,561.46kg),

had a hull shape higher and wider than that of the T-34, with a large, set-back turret to accommodate the long-barreled 7.5cm KwK (*KampfwagenKanone*) 42, *Leichter* (calibre) (L/70) gun. Its internal layout followed the normal protocols of German tank design and power was supplied by a V-12 Maybach HL 210 P30 petrol engine, a seven-speed synchromesh gearbox, with the drive leading to front sprockets, torsion bar suspension and inter-leaved roadwheels.

Initially Hitler favoured the Daimler-Benz design, although he felt it should have a more

9

Both pages:
A captured Panther on trials in England — note the ballast weights bolted to the vehicle. Interestingly, the hull is that of an Ausf D whilst the turret is from an Ausf A. The tank is one of those designated, by the Germans, an Ausf A (D1). The turret carries the number 433 whilst on the left rear are the words, in white paint, M.I.10 LONDON and WAR OFF. *(TM)*

Above:
A Panther Ausf D of the 15th Panzer Division on its training area at Sagan, Silesia. *(TM)*

Right:
A knocked-out Panther Ausf A(D1) at Bastogne. The tank has the Ausf D chassis and the later Ausf A turret. *(TM)*

owerful gun. This led to an order being
placed for 200 of the VK 3002(DB) model.
However, the *Heereswaffenamt* preferred the
MAN design, particularly because the MB 507
diesel engine proposed by Daimler-Benz had
never been tested, while the new gun which
Hitler wanted could never be fitted into the
vehicle's small turret. It therefore asked MAN
to produce a mild steel prototype as quickly as
possible - which was ready by September 1942
and trialled on the works' testing grounds at
Nuremberg (Nürnberg). A second prototype,
completed soon afterwards, went for testing at
the *Heereswaffenamt* testing grounds at
Kummersdorf. Ing Kniepkamp, the chief
engineer and designer of *Waffenprüfamt VI*, had
taken personal charge of the detailed design
work on the MAN model and the project was
given top priority, being moved forward
therefore with great urgency.

As a result of these trials the MAN design
was chosen for production over its rival, the
Daimler-Benz order being cancelled, but the

company later became a major contractor.
The new vehicle was ordered into immediate
production and given the designation *Panzer
Kampfwagen V* (PzKpfw V) and the *WaPrüf*
designation *SonderKraftfahrzeug* (SdKfz)171,
although unofficially known as Panther. To
begin with it was planned to produce 250 tanks
a month, then, at the end of 1942, this target was
raised to 600. Clearly MAN could not handle
such a large order alone and so Daimler-Benz
was also contracted for Panther production.
Other companies joined the production group
later, either as main producers (MNH
[Maschinenfabrik Niedersachsen of Hannover],
Henschel and later Demag) or as sub-
contractors for engines and other components.

In mid-July 1941, Rheinmetall-Borsig had
been given a contract to develop a tank main
gun which could penetrate 5.52in (140mm) of
armour at 1,090yd (1,000m). At the same time
it was also authorised to design a turret for the
VK 3002 project, to take the new gun. By early
1942 it had produced a test barrel - the L/60 -

Above:
An abandoned
Ausf A being
examined by US Army
troops. The tank is
fitted with side
armour plates
(*Schürzen*) and is
coated with *Zimmerit*,
anti-magnetic mine
paste. Note at the rear
of the vehicle there is
a box (probably
manufactured in the
field) in which is
carried a Jerrican for
fuel or water. *(TM)*

but the performance did not reach the required specification, so a L/70 barrel length was chosen and delivery fixed for June 1942. This target date was met and the gun went into full production, initially with a single muzzle brake, which was later changed to a double-baffle type. It was a gun of superlative performance and deservedly feared by Allied and Soviet tank crews.

Ausf A (D1)

The first 20 Panthers to come off the production line at MAN from November 1942 onwards were designated Ausf A in the normal German manner, although this designation was later retroactively changed to Ausf D1. They were built to the basic design specifications which the VK 3002 project had demanded, with all armour being sloped other than the lower hull sides. The vehicle had armour of 2.36in (60mm) upper and 1.58in (40mm) lower thickness on the glacis or front plate and 1.58in (40mm) on the sides, and a V-12 Maybach HL 210 P30 petrol engine providing the required 25-35mph (40-55km/h), with a ZF type AK7-200 gearbox, dry clutch linked to the standard-type brake steering. This model mounted the earliest type of the KwK 42 (L/70) main gun in an external curved, cast mantlet, along with a coaxial 7.92mm MG 34 machine gun which did not actually protrude through the mantlet. The sloping, angular turret had a high, bin-shaped cupola mounted on the roof in the rear left corner. The turret walls had pistol ports in each of the sides and one at the rear. There was also an escape hatch at the turret rear and an ammunition loading hatch on the left side. It could be said that these original 20 Ausf As were really pre-production models, as they did not have any of the design improvements which had been proposed following the trials of pilot models.

The Ausf B was to have been a Panther fitted with the Maybach Olvar eight-speed gearbox instead of the ZF type AK7-200, but this proved unsatisfactory and so the designation was never used. What happened to the designation Ausf C remains a mystery, but it was presumably allocated to another model which never left the drawing board, so the first full production model was designated Ausf D.

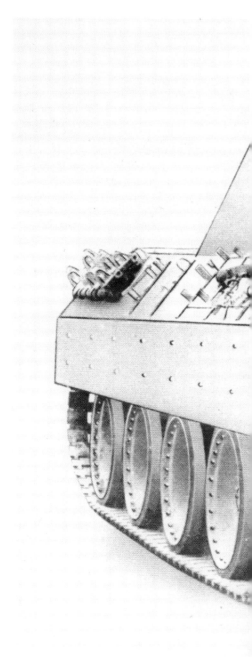

To try to keep the records straight the initial Ausf A batch was later given the designation Ausf D1, while the Ausf D was sometimes known as the Ausf D2.

Ausf D

The Ausf D incorporated various design improvements, beginning with thicker armour

The glacis was increased to 3.15in (80mm) upper and 2.36in (60mm) lower, with 1.58in (40mm) on the sides and rear, .63in (16mm) on the hull roof and 1.18in (30mm) in the floor. The turret armour was increased to 3.94in (100mm) on the front, with the mantlet also of a similar thickness: 1.58in (40mm) sides and rear and .63in (16mm) on its roof. Thus the Ausf D's combat weight increased to 43 tons (43,689.79kg), although through improvements to the engine its top speed, 28mph (46km/h),

and range, 124 miles (200km), remained the same. The vehicle's dimensions were: length: 29.07ft (8.86m); width: 11.15ft (3.4m) and height: 9.68ft (2.95m). Its main armament was the long-barrelled 7.5cm *KampfwagenKanone 42*(kwK 42), a 70-calibre (L/70) tank-killing gun with a single-baffle muzzle brake, mounted in the moving mantlet in the turret with a 7.92mm MG 34 coaxial machine gun, with hydraulic and hand traverse. Early Ausf D models still retained the bin-shaped cupola of the

Above:
A 'factory fresh' Ausf A, note the new-shape turret and cupola. The tank is fitted with equipment panniers at the rear. *(TM)*

Right:
On the Ausf A, the letter-box-type MG port was deleted and replaced by an armoured ball-mount for the MG 34. The driver's vision port has been retained in the glacis. Only one headlight is fitted and this has a blackout mask. *(TM)*

arly Ausf A (D1), but later D models were produced with a new type of cupola. Instead of the round, flat-topped housing with six vision lits and a hinged lid, the new type consisted of a more domed shape, with seven periscope owls (usually surmounted by a flat ring for an AA gun attachment) and a dished plate turret id, which had first to be raised and then swung out to the left-hand side. The cupola was also moved slightly to the right to make the turret tronger and production easier by not touching he turret wall. There were smoke dischargers positioned on the front at both turret sides. There was no hull machine gun mount in the glacis plate but the wireless operator/bow gunner did have a letterbox-style gun port et into the right-hand side of the glacis in front of his station. The vehicle's engine capacity was now raised from 21,350cc (650hp) o 23,880cc (700hp) by enlarging the cylinder bore, the engine then being known as the HL 230 P 30, which produced 700bhp, passing hrough a Zahnradfabrik Friedrichshafen ZF) AK7-200 seven-speed gearbox to the ransmission and the track drives, controlled by

a new brake/steering system. Track suspension remained the twin torsion bar type, with (on each track) eight pairs of interleaved bogie wheels sprung on torsion bars, a front drive sprocket and a rear idler.

Three companies - MAN, Daimler-Benz, and Henschel - were now producing the Ausf D, some 800 being built between January and September 1943. Unfortunately, as the production had been so rushed at the *Führer's* insistence, these early Panthers suffered from numerous mechanical faults, especially to their transmission and steering, which, having been originally designed for lighter tanks, was not really up to the stresses caused by the vehicle's increased weight and the power of the larger engine. The same also applied to the engine itself, which was overloaded and thus prone to overheating - often causing fires. Having been rushed into combat with much hype for Operation *Zitadelle* (Citadel), the German offensive at Kursk, the Panther was a deep disappointment for the troops who first used it, although its armament had clearly proven itself - knocking out a T-34 at a range of over

Above:
Constructed from wood, the Germans positioned many of these dummy Panthers in Normandy. When covered with branches and camouflage netting they presented the realistic angular shape of the Panther. *(TM)*

Right:
New Panther Ausf Ds awaiting delivery to Panzer units from the Maschinenfabrik Niedersachsen - Hannover. Production began at the company in February 1943. *(TM)*

7,665yd (7,000m). They were therefore recalled for modification and as these automotive teething problems were ironed out the Panther would go on to greater things.

Ausf A

The next production model was for some reason designated as Ausf A instead of the expected Ausf E - obviously the Panther nomenclature sequence followed some arcane proceedure of the *Heeereswaffenamt*. It first appeared in August 1943 and some 2,000 were built by four companies - Henschel, MAN, Daimler-Benz and MNH - up until May 1945. Its basic design and automotive components remained the same as the previous model, but improvements continued to be made to the drive-train as well as other modifications based on battle experience from the Eastern front. In this way, though the weight of the vehicle rose slightly to 44.8 tons (45,518.66kg), its top speed, 28mph (46km/h), and range 124 miles (200km) did not decrease.

The Ausf A had fractionally larger dimensions than its predecessor - length: 29.07ft (8.86m); width: 11.22ft (3.42m) and height: 9.80ft (2.98m). Its hull armour remained the same as before - front: 3.15in (80mm) upper and 2.36in (60mm) lower, with 1.58in (40mm) on the sides and rear, .63in (16mm) on the hull roof and 1.18in (30mm) in the floor. The turret however was uparmoured by some .39in (10mm) at the front, making 4.33in (110mm), with the mantlet remaining 3.94in(100mm); 1.58in (40mm) sides and rear and .63in (16mm) on the turret roof. The main armament remained the long-barrelled 7.5cm KwK 42 (L/70), though fitted with a new double-baffled muzzle brake. The hull machine gun (7.92mm MG 34) was now given a ball-mounting, set in the glacis to replace the previous letterbox-type opening. The engine exhaust and cooling system was modified and the number of retaining bolts on the wheels were doubled to prevent failures. The turret underwent extensive modification, beginning with the improved cupola with better vision through armoured episcopes rather than vision slits that had been standard up until into the late production Ausf Ds, along with the addition of an exterior ring on

the cupola to mount another MG 34. There was now an improved sight for the gunner a Leitz of Wetzlar TZF12A monocular telescope, replacing the older TZF12 binocular telescope - and also the provision of a roof mounted periscope for the loader. Other change

included the elimination of the ammunition loading hatch on the left-hand side and the removal of the pistol ports in the sides and rear in preference for the *Nahverteidigungswaffe* (close-in defence weapon). These modifications made a stronger, more simplified turret.

The Ausf A saw action on primarily the Eastern front, but also in southern Italy and western Europe following the Normandy landings, as well as the last German offensive of the war, the Battle of the Bulge, the winter attack in the Ardennes.

Ausf G

The final production model of the Panther was the Ausf G and it continued to reflect changes recommended through battle experience. This model was built in larger quantities than any of the others, over 3,000 being constructed between March 1944 and April 1945 by MAN, Daimler-Benz and MNH. Its dimensions were the same as the previous Panther, Ausf A; length: 29.07ft (8.86m); width: 11.22ft (3.42m) and height: 9.80ft (2.98m) and its armour thickness remained the same other than a fractional increase in the sides and floor of the hull: front: 3.15in (80mm) upper and 2.36in (60mm) lower, with 1.97in (50mm) on the sides and rear, .63in (16mm) on the hull roof and 1.58in (40mm) the floor. The turret remained at 3.94in (110mm) front, with the mantlet 3.94in (100mm), 1.58in (40mm) sides and rear and .63in (16mm) on the turret roof, and the main gun and coaxial MG were as before: the KwK 42 (L/70) and 7.92mm MG 34. However, the construction of the hull actually underwent a redesign, beginning with more sloping, thicker side armour and with the sides now being made from a single plate. The front glacis was strengthened by the removal of the driver's vision port, which was replaced by a rotating periscope in the roof of the hull above his compartment. The hatches for the driver and hull gunner were improved by making them hinged, rather than swinging on pivots, and they were also fitted with springs to make them still easier to open. The driver could now extend his seat and driving control levers to drive the tank while looking out of his hatch when not closed down for combat.

Vehicle suspension also remained the same as the Ausf A, except that on late production models the rear damper was removed. On the final production versions of the Ausf G the drive train continued to be improved, the ZF type AK7-200 gearbox was replaced, on a few vehicles, by the eight-speed AK7-400 and there was a gearbox oil cooler fitted to ease the strain on the mechanism. This helps explain while although increasing in all-up weight to 45.5 tons (46,229.98kg), the Ausf G attained the same speed, 28mph (46km/h), and range, 124 miles (200km) as previous models, while becoming still more reliable. Distinctive bulbous flame trap exhaust mufflers were fitte at the back of the vehicle and there were ne resilient steel roadwheels provided, along with new method of attaching the .20in (5mm *Schürzen* (skirting) armour plates.

Changes to the turret included th provision of a turret heating system using he generated by the main engine. Ammunitio stowage was increased from 79 to 82 round with .12in (3mm) armoured stowage bin provided in panniers located on the slopin superstructure sides.

The gun mantlet was also modified t prevent shots being deflected down into th

hinly armoured hull roof (this had happened with disastrous results), by the squaring-off of ts bottom curve.

The designation of this last model was now changed to Panther Ausf G, the PzKpfw V part of its previous designation being dropped altogether following a directive from the *Führer* dated 27 February 1944.

Both infrared night sights and a stabiliser system for the main armament were planned for the Ausf G, but they were not produced in ime for operational use before the war's end.

This model saw action on both eastern, southern and western European fronts,

including being disguised with the addition of metal plates to modify the turret silhouette replicating US Army M10 tank destroyers in the final Ardennes offensive. Specific model identification can sometimes be tricky between the Ausf A and G models, for, as with all German armour, tanks coming in for repairs were often updated with the latest modifications to their series.

The Ausf F was to have been the next model, but it never went into production, although a few prototype hulls were produced in 1945. It was to have had the same basic specifications as previous models, although it

Above:
Panther Ausf G, the final production model fitted with the extremely powerful, 7.5cm KwK 42 L/70 gun, now with a double-baffle muzzle brake. The driver's vision slot has been deleted from the glacis. *(GF)*

Right:
The hull/superstructure assembly shop for Ausf G at the MNH factory, Hannover. The machine in the top centre appears to be a jig welder for joining the lower hull to the super-structure. Also on the line is the hull/superstructure assembly for a JgdPz V (SdKfz 173) Jagdpanther. *(TM)*

Above:
A Panther Ausf A being recovered from a damaged building after the Normandy landings, 6 June 1944. The US Army personnel are using a Kenworth M1A1 heavy wrecker to aid with the work. The tank carries the number, in white, 413 on the turret sides. *(TM)*

was to have been uparmoured to: front: 3.15in (80mm) upper and 2.36in (60mm) lower, with 1.58in (40mm) on the sides and rear, .98in (25mm) on the hull roof and 1.18in (30mm) the floor. A new considerably smaller turret was redesigned by Daimler-Benz. Called the *Schmalturm* (narrow turret), it was to have mounted a stabilised sight with range finder bulges on its sides and a 8.8cm KwK 43 (L/71) main gun. The armour turret thickness was to have been increased by some .39in (10mm) at the front, making 4.73in (120mm), with the mantlet - also a new design called *Saukopfblende* (pig's head) - increased by .39in (10mm), to 4.73in (120mm); and with a .59in (15mm) increase to 2.36in (60mm) to the sides and rear and a large increase from .63in (16mm) on the turret roof to 1.58in (40mm). Other changes included the replacement of the hull MG 34 with a new type, the MP 44, more radio equipment and the provision of an AA machine gun mounted on the cupola.

Panther II was the major upgrade planned for the Panther, but again never went beyond the prototype stage. In April 1942 th Heereswaffenamt commissioned both MAN an Henschel to work jointly on a project t upgrade the Panther and the Tiger, trying t achieve as much parts commonality as possibl between the two tanks, in order to mak production and maintenance simpler. Of th two designs, Tiger II went on to be produced but the Panther II never got beyond th prototype stage. It was essentially to have bee the same as the Panther I, but at 50 ton (50,802kg) considerably heavier.

Variants that were actually built included th *Panzerbefehlswagen* (SdKfz179) (SdKfz 267/8 (PzBefWg) Command Tank and the *Panzer beobachtungswagen* (SdKfz 179) (PzBeobWg Observation Post Tank. Three hundred an thirty Panthers were converted to the comman role from May 1943 to February 1945 and 40 t the observation role in late 1944/early 1945 Both vehicles' specifications remained the sam as other Panther models except for specifi addition or deletion of certain equipmen dictated by each vehicle's role.

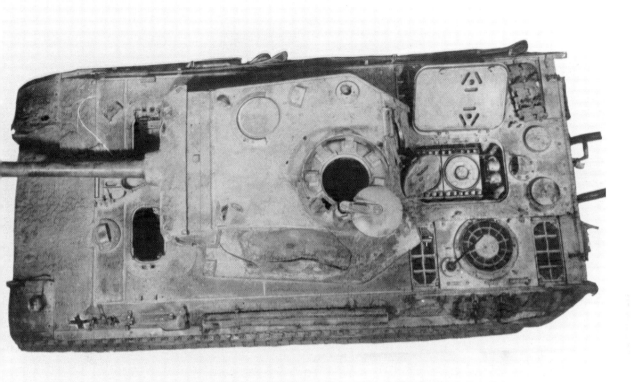

The PzBefWg Command Tank was developed to appear exactly the same as any other Panther when in action, with the additional radio fitted by reducing the amount of main gun ammunition carried. The usual FuG5 radio was fitted in the turret and the extra FuG7 or FuG8 communications necessary for the command function were installed in the hull above the gearbox. The PzBeoWg, Observation Post Tank was converted by removing the mantlet/main gun assembly then plating over the hole, before fitting a smaller wooden dummy mantlet and dummy main gun, whilst keeping the turret 7.92mm MG 34. Both vehicles mounted extra aerials - a star-type antenna in the centre of the rear deck and a rod aerial on the right side of the turret roof as well as the usual FuG5 aerial behind and to the left of the turret on the rear deck.

Another variant, the *Jagdpanther* (SdKfz 173), was a heavy tank destroyer using the Panther chassis, manufactured by MIAG (Mühlenbau und Industrie AG) and MNH, with approximately 400 being produced

between January 1944 and March 1945. It had a crew of five, the same Maybach HL 230 P30 engine and ZF type AK-400 transmission, a speed of 28mph (46km/h) and a range of 99 miles (160km). Its dimensions were - length: 32.48ft (9.9m); width: 11.22ft (3.42m) and height: 8.92ft (2.72m) and it weighed 46 tons (46,737.91kg). Armour was a follows - hull front: 2.36in (60mm); sides and rear: 1.58in (40mm); with a superstructure of front glacis plate:3.15in (80mm); sides: 1.97in (50mm); rear 1.58in (40mm) and roof .98in (25mm). Its main armament was the 8.8cm *Fliegerabwehr Kanone* (FlaK) 43/3 (L/71) in a *Saukopfblende* (pig's head) mantlet set into the front glacis plate, with a ball-mounted 7.92mm MG 34 in the glacis beside it - but not coaxial with the main gun. The size of the vehicle's fighting compartment was increased by extending the upper hull and side plates of the normal Panther chassis.

Another variant was the *Bergepanzerwagen-Panther* (SdKfz 179) or *Bergepanther* - an armoured recovery vehicle for heavy tanks,

Above:
A superb overhead view of an Ausf G showing access hatches. Unfortunately the driver's and gunner's hatches have been removed from the tank. Note also the heavy shell damage to the side of the turret. *(TM)*

Above:
Panther Ausf A *Panzerbefehlswagen* (Command Tank) bearing the markings of the 116th Panzer Lehr Division.

Right:
Prototype for the Ausf D *Panzerbefehls-wagen*. Note the distinctive three radio antennae mounted on the tank – one on the turret, two on the engine compartment deck. *(TM)*

use in Italy as strongpoints in the static defences of the Hitler and Gothic lines, often being a salient feature around which the other defences were positioned and they proved very effective, being difficult to destroy. They were mounted on a turret ring which was fitted to a welded armoured box of approximately 2.5in (63mm) thickness. The box (which also provided living quarters for the crew) was then sunk into the ground and earth was banked up and around, making it almost invisible. Access to the turret was either through the cupola turret door or else from underneath – where the crew lived via a steel ladder. The crew entered the box through an aperture at the rear.

uilt by MAN, Henschel and Demag from June 943 until September 1944. Most had the same pecifications as the Ausf A in terms of engine Maybach HL230P30), all-up weight 43 tons 43,689.79kg), speed 28mph (46km/h) and rmour as for the Ausf D; it had an increased ange of 198 miles (320km) and no turret; nstead, two 1.5-ton (1,524kg) capacity square-ection wooden derricks were fitted (the tandard German ARV [Armoured Recovery Vehicle] equipment), along with other ngineering and pioneer tools. The only rmament carried by the *Bergepanther* was a 0mm KwK (FlaK) 38 L/55 cannon.

The Panther chassis was also used to develop series of anti-aircraft and self-propelled rtillery vehicles, none of which was ready for ervice by May 1945.

Surplus Panther Ausf D turrets also saw

Production

In total 5,508 Panther and Bergepanthers were built, eventually becoming the most important tank on the production lines – two Panthers could be built in the same number of man hours required to build a single Tiger. It was to have been the basic main battle tank of the *Panzerwaffe*, but in the end the firmly established PzKpfw IV kept that role, though Panthers were issued to an increasing number of regiments as more were produced. This excellent tank went some way towards redressing the balance that had tipped against the Germans, although their failure was more fundamental and primarily strategic. As the Allies closed in, tank chassis were diverted off the production lines to produce more heavily defensive armour, such as self-propelled artillery. In the final analysis German production of war material could not compete with the combined Allied industrial capability, with precious resources also being wasted on huge, impractical weapon variants like the *Maus* (Mouse), initiated by the *Führer*, with his increasingly desperate and catastrophic interference. Although Panther was an excellent offensive vehicle, fast for its time, with a very powerful gun and a strongly armoured front, it suffered (like all German tanks built for war the 'other way' into western Europe) from having an overcomplicated engine and transmission, too narrow tracks, complicated transmission and running gear that required much maintenance.

The Panther was designed to be built on the progressive batch production line system.

Above:
An Ausf D chassis fitted as a *Panzerbeobachtungswagen* (Observation Post Tank) for artillery spotting. The turret front has been plated over and fitted with a ball-mounted MG 34. The main gun and mantlet are dummy, being fabricated in wood. The turret did not traverse. *(GF)*

Right:
The artillery spotter's range plotting turntable mounted in the fighting compartment. *(TM)*

Above:
The binocular range finder telescope fitted in the turret roof. *(TM)*

Left:
A petrol-powered auxiliary generator, fitted at the rear of the fighting compartment, provided back-up electric power for more radio and other equipment. *(TM)*

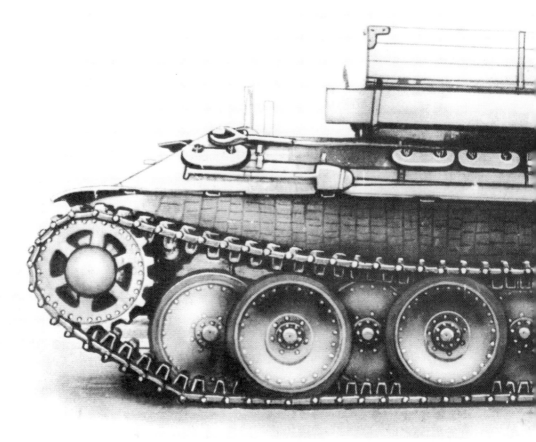

Above:
A total of 297
Bergepanzer-Panther
(SdKfz 179) Ausf A,
also known as
the *Bergepanther*,
were developed by
Demag of Berlin-
Falkensee and built by
it and MNH from
armour supplied by
Ruhrstahl of
Hattingen. *(GF)*

Right:
The *Bergepanther* was
fitted with a powerful
winch mounted in the
turretless fighting
compartment. Note
the spade lowered
to prevent the
vehicle sliding
when recovering
a vehicle. *(TM)*

30

Below:
The *Bergepanther* was the only armoured recovery vehicle (ARV) capable of towing a Panther or Tiger. The only armament fitted to the tank was a 20mm KwK (FlaK) 38 L/55 cannon. The vehicle was powered by a V-12 Maybach HL 230 P30 engine but was fitted with improved transmission – a ZF type AK7-400 seven-speed gearbox. Range was improved by increasing fuel capacity to 236.5gals (1,075 litres). A few *Bergepanthers* were converted, by removing the winch and spade, in the field to *Munitionspanzer-Panther* ammunitions carrier. *(TM)*

Above:
Rear of an Ausf G. Note the equipment panniers each side and the 'field manufactured' box on the engine deck which usually carried extra Jerricans of fuel or water. The various hatches on the back plate allowed access to the engine compartment for the inertia starter and track tensioners. *(TM)*

Companies that produced Panther and its variants were:

Maschinenfabrik Ausgburg-Nürnberg (MAN)
Daimler Benz, Berlin - Marienfelde
Maschinenfabrik Niedersachsen of Hanover (MNH)
Demag, Berlin-Falkensee
Henschel, Kassel
Mühlenbau und Industrie AG (MIAG), Brunswick

Rheinmetal Borsig of Berlin-Tegel made all the main guns and Panther production was also begun further east, as the Germans availed themselves of conquered countries' industrial assets. In Polish Upper Silesia, Panther construction was begun following the capture of three important steelworks - Königshütte for electric steel, Bismarckhütte for electric steel and

rolled homogeneous armour and Bankhütte for mechanical engineering and hull/super structure fabrication. Considerable expansion of production was planned but never realised before the end of the war.

Production

1943	1768	} by Henschel, MAN and Daimler-Benz (later MNH)
1944/45	3740	
total	5508	
Pz Bergepanther		
1943	82	} by MNH and Demag
1944/45	215	
total	297	

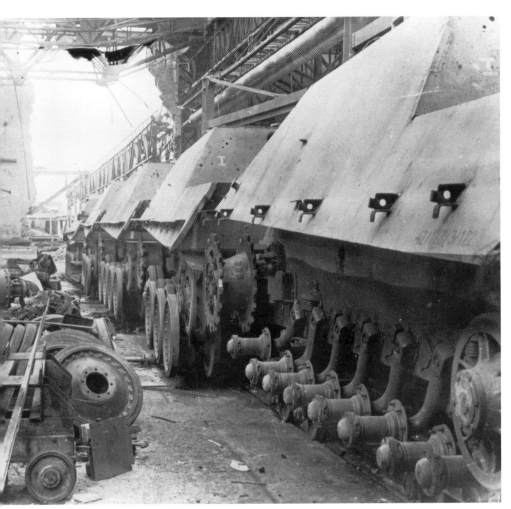

Left:
Jagdpanthers (Jagdpz V [SdKfz 173]) on the production line at MNH, Hannover. Note the suspension arms before the fitting of the road wheels. *(TM)*

Below:
The might *Jagdpanther*, considered by many the best tank hunter/killer of World War Two. *(TM) (This and other Panzerjägers in German service are to be covered in a later book in this series.)*

Above and right:
During the Battle of the Bulge, four Panther Ausf Gs were disguised with added thin metal plate to give them the appearance of the US Armys' M-10 Hellcat tank destroyer. The tanks were used by Otto Skorzeny's Panzer Brigade 150 as a US uniformed unit. All four were subsequently destroyed in the battle. *(TM)*

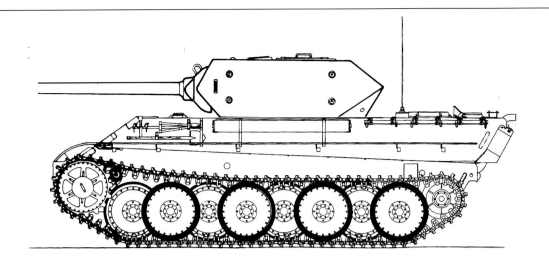

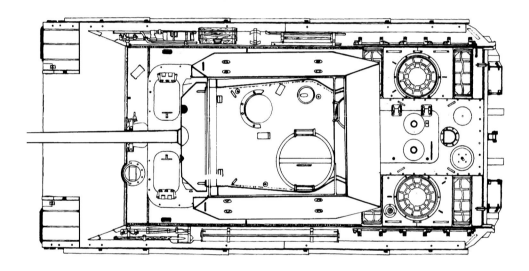

The Ausf G Panther disguised, in the field,
as a US Army M-10 Hellcat tank destroyer.

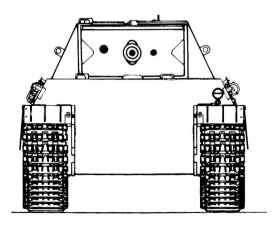

© Hilary Louise Doyle 2003.

Right:
Surplus Ausf D turrets were used in Italy to provide defensive strongpoints. The turret was mounted on a fabricated steel box (which served as the crew's living quarters) fitted with a standard turret race. Gun traversing and elevation were by manual operation. Once the box was sited, earth was banked up and around to conceal its location. *(TM)*

Below:
The turret mounting box set up on a framework of logs before being covered with earth. Note the crew's entry door. *(TM)*

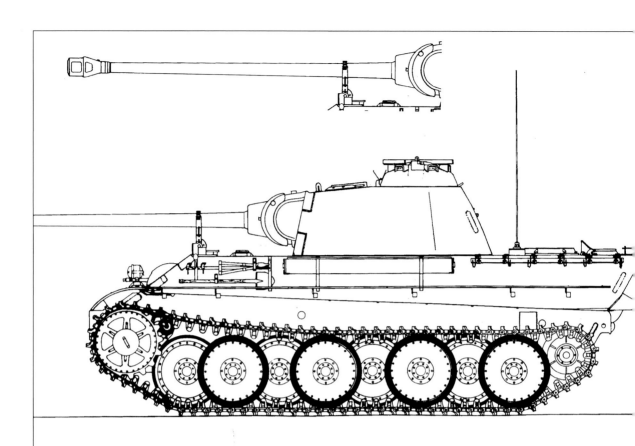

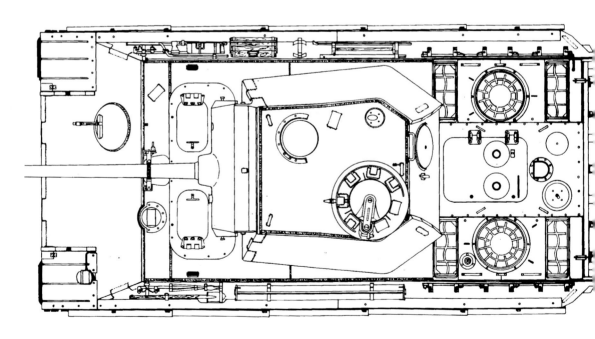

PanzerKampfwagen V (SdKfz171) Panther Ausf G

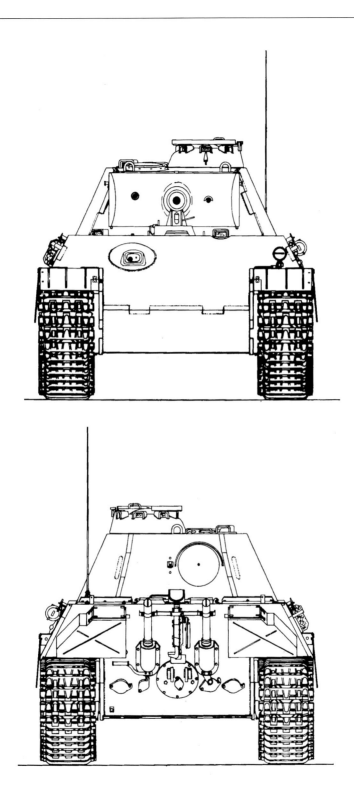

17 pounder firing A.P.C.B.C. at 2900 F/S

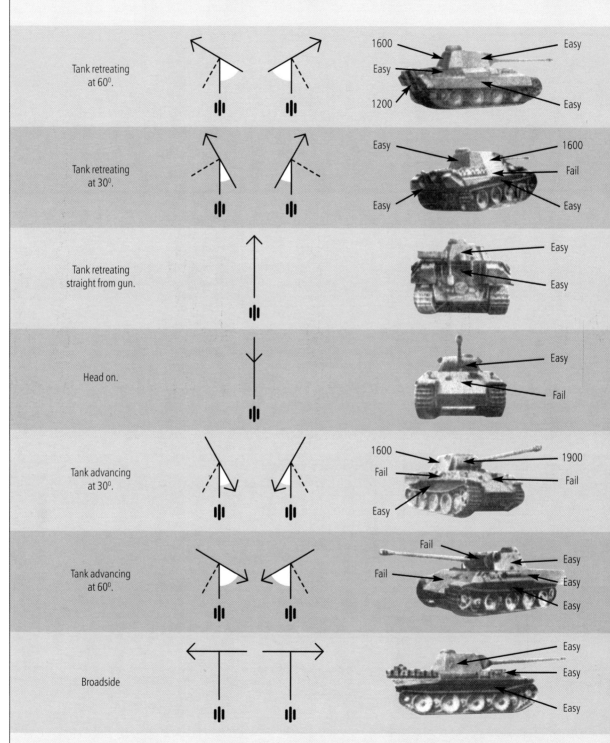

The arrows show the direction in which the tank is moving.
The numbers show the range in yards at which the plates indicated can be perforated under the particular conditions.
The word "easy" denotes that the critical range has been assessed at more than 2500 yards.

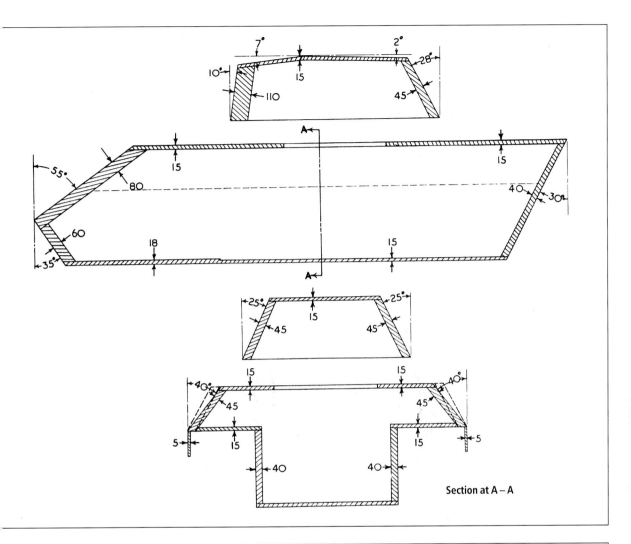

Section at A – A

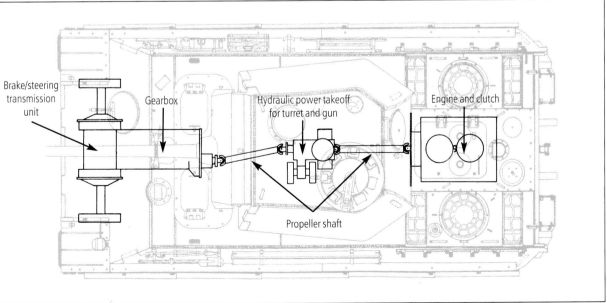

Brake/steering transmission unit

Gearbox

Hydraulic power takeoff for turret and gun

Engine and clutch

Propeller shaft

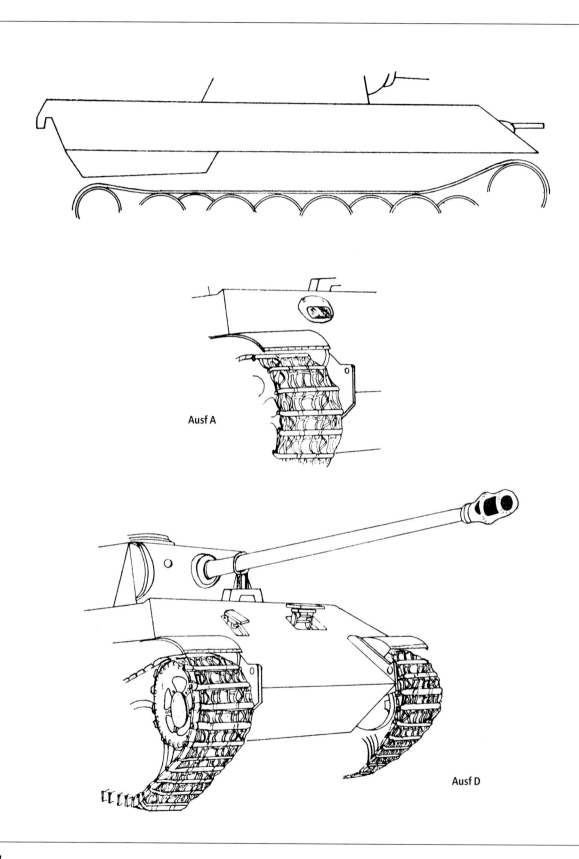

Ausf A

Ausf D

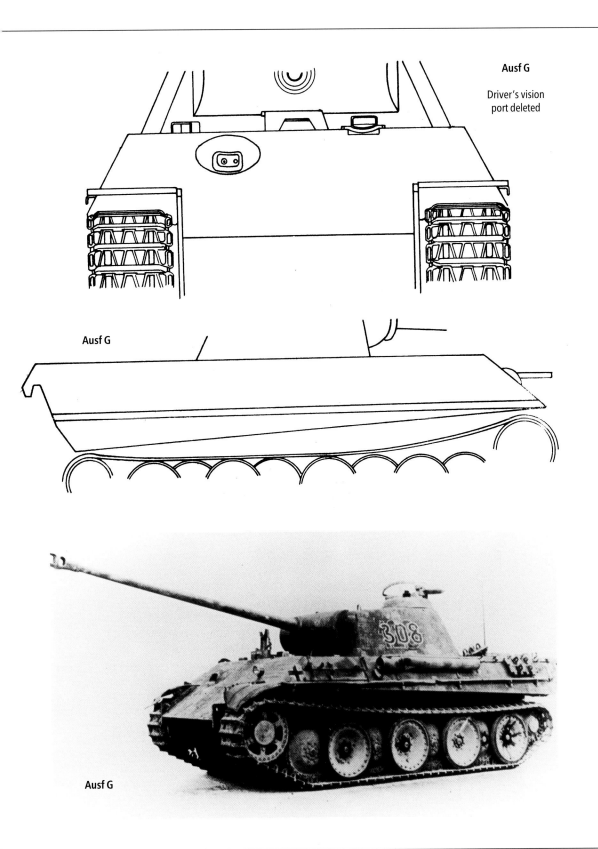

Ausf G

Driver's vision
port deleted

Ausf G

Ausf G

CHAPTER TWO

CHASSIS, ENGINE & TRACKS

The Panther was the first German tank designed to have
an all–welded integral hull and superstructure assembly,
which changed only in small detail and armour thickness.
Engine power was provided, as in most German tanks, by
Maybach with the V–12 HL 210 P30 or HL 230 P30.

With its design based on the Soviet T34, which it was built to defeat, the Panther had some new characteristics which it shared with its enemy and others which followed the normal direction of German tank design and construction techniques. The main feature that it shared (and took) from the T-34 was its sloping armour. This increased the effective horizontal thickness of the armoured plates without any corresponding increase in weight and so offered a more difficult angle to attack. Another novel feature in the T-34 design, as far as the Germans were concerned, was that the hull and superstructure were fabricated as a single unit rather than bolted together. The interlocking plates and stop-welded joint construction, first developed for the PzKpfw VI Tiger, were also used on the Panther to give the hull assembly greater rigidity. This involved the armoured plates being made to interlock with special steps cut at the joints so as to act as seats for the welds, thereby considerably further strengthening the joint.

The tank was built in two parts - hull/superstructure and turret - with construction being straightforward using rolled homogenous armoured steel plate, seam-welded inside and out apart from the cast mantlet and cupola. The

topsides of the hull extended out over the track, being wider in the centre section, to facilitate the fitting of a large-diameter turret ring and therefore a larger turret - a standard feature of German tank design.

The overall measurements of the Panther series changed only fractionally by a few centimetres in width and height, but not in length. Ausf D - length: 29.07ft (8.86m); width 11.15ft (3.4m) and height: 9.68ft (2.95m). Ausf and G - length: 29.07ft (8.86m); width: 11.22 (3.42m) and height: 9.78ft (2.98m).

The vehicle's armour saw various increase as the series progressed - the inevitable up armouring that almost all German AFV underwent during their combat life. The thickness of the glacis increased from 2.36i (60mm) to 3.15in (80mm), the hull sides from 1.58in (40mm) to 1.97in (50mm), the hull roo from 1.18in (30mm) to 1.58in (40mm). Turre armour was also increased.

Unlike the more usual angular appearance o German tanks, following the Soviet T-34's mor simplified smoother design, the Panther hull wa sloped in a similar fashion on the front glaci giving the vehicle a distinctive angular shape Although wide, the superstructure was not deep

Above:
Railway wagons loaded with Panther Ausf As on their way to the Normandy battlefront. *(TM)*

Left:
A specially designed machine for locating and fitting the bearings for the torsion bar suspension. The Ausf G's hull assembly is held on a jig whilst the machine heads move along the length of the vehicle. *(TM)*

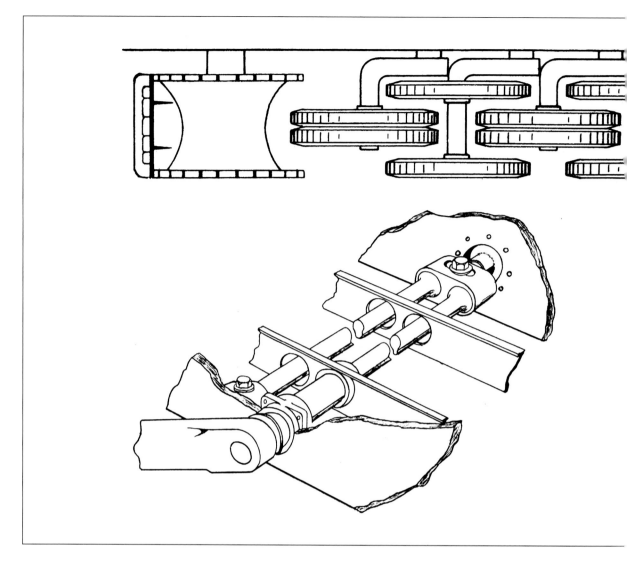

and it rode rather high above the wheels and tracks - appearing higher towards the back where an additional smaller, deeper plate was often welded, tapering inwards and backwards. This was partly because the front-drive sprocket on each side was almost level with the bottom of the upper glacis plate, higher than the other wheels, the effect being countered on later models with the reversion to straight side plates running the length of the hull. Cut into the glacis were, on the Ausf D, a vertical letterbox-type gun port for the radio operator/hull gunner and a square vision port for the driver. This strange-shaped gun port was changed on the next model (Ausf A) to the more familiar machine gun ball mount, and, in order not to compromise the strength of the glacis, the driver's port was also deleted on later versions. This was replaced by a periscope-type

vision port mounted in the driver's hatch. The superstructure front was part of the glacis plate, where there was a headlight fitted on the driver side (sometimes on both sides), and detachable mudguard-type plates providing access to the running gear were fitted at the front, curving downwards protectively over the tracks. On each side at the front of the angled sides of the superstructure, elliptical-shaped towing shackles were fitted. Also mounted on the sides were pioneer tools, track links, track repair kit, main gun cleaning equipment (stored in a long metal cylinder) and a heavy hawser for towing. Slightly off centre towards the front, steel rungs were set vertically, to aid with access onto the vehicle, with one rung sometimes also welded horizontally on the bottom of the lower side plate. At the rear of the tank twin exhausts exited upwards above the

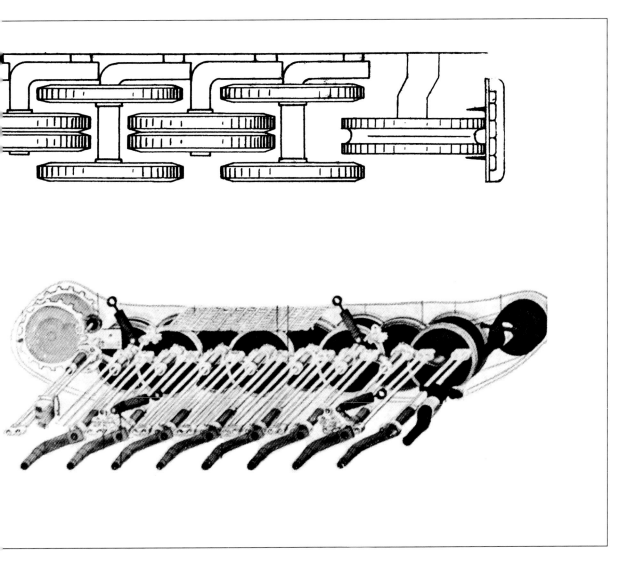

back deck (larger diameter and longer on later versions with the addition of anti-flame flaps), and there were also several engine accesss ports. There were also access hatches beneath the engine, in the hull floor. The reason that so much equipment was carried on the sides of the vehicle was that the space behind the turret was taken up with fans, air inlet grilles and access panels and ports to the engine. The aerial radio antenna base was also on the back deck, mounted to the left, behind the turret.

Internally, the Panther conformed to the standard layout of German tanks with the driver's compartment at the front, the fighting compartment in the centre and the engine at the rear. In the front compartment the gearbox was mounted just off centre, to the right, with seats on either side - on the left for the driver

and on the right for the radio operator/hull gunner. The driver's position was fitted with a vision port (replaced by a periscope on the Ausf G) directly in front of him in the glacis plate, fitted with an *Ersatzgläser* (safety glass) block and an armoured cover which measured 9.76in (24.8cm) by 3.94in (10 cm) that was operated by a single spring-loaded lever. When driving closed down the driver used two fixed episcopes in the roof of the compartment, one facing directly forward at 12 on the clock scale, the other half-facing left at 10 o'clock. Visibility was not good, so the advent of the fully rotating periscope in the Ausf G was a welcome modification. The driver had the usual controls with the gear lever on the right and handbrake on the left, plus an instrument panel (with speedometer, rev counter, oil pressure

Above:
This illustration of the Panther's suspension system is taken from an original *Panzerwaffe* manual. On later Ausf Gs the rear two hydraulic dampers were deleted. *(TM)*

gauge and ammeter). There was also a button on the panel for the electric starter. During very cold weather or if the vehicle's batteries were low a *Durchdrehenanlasser* (inertia starter) located in the engine compartment could be used, the crank handle being inserted through the rear hull plate. Two men were needed to swing the handle - later models were fitted with an improved (starting system) which was easier to operate.

The radio operator/hull gunner sat on the right of the driving compartment by the side of the gearbox. The gunner manned an MG 34 which was fired through the vertical letterbox-type flap in the glacis plate. On later models this was replaced by an MG 34 in a *Kugelblende* (ball mounting), which also incorporated a sighting aperture. To the gunner's right, fitted into the sponson, was all the radio equipment, while in the hatch above were similar fixed periscopes to that for the driver. Both had large oblong escape hatches which opened by first raising slightly, then swivelling outwards (hinged and spring-assisted in the Ausf G).

The bearers for the engine gearbox, drive units and fuel tanks were all welded in place, as was the mounting for the fighting compartment's rotating floor. A circular escape hatch was cut into the floor on the right-hand side ahead of the forward bulkhead and there was a large engine inspection/access hatch in the centre of the rear compartment wall.

The engine planned for the Ausf D Panther was the Maybach HL 210 P30 but in service this was found to be not powerful enough for this heavier than previous tanks. In later Ausf Ds a more powerful HL 230 P30 was fitted and became the standard engine for subsequent Ausf A and G production.

Engine Specification:

Ausf D (early model)

Engine:	MAYBACH HL 210 P30
Cylinders:	V-12 at 60⁰
Capacity:	21,350cc (21.35ltr)
Horsepower:	650 at 3,000rpm
Carburettors:	Four SOLEX 40JFF2 downdraught type
Ignition:	Two Bosch JGN6R18 magnetos
Cooling:	Liquid 70% glycol/water

Ausf D (later model) Ausf A and Ausf G

Engine:	MAYBACH HL 230 P30
Cylinders:	V-12 at 60⁰
Capacity:	23,880cc (23.88ltr)
Horsepower:	700 at 3,000rpm
Carburettors:	Four SOLEX 52FFJ downdraught type
Ignition:	Two Bosch JGN6R18 magnetos
Cooling:	Liquid 70% glycol/water

Note: HL (*Hochleistungs-motor*), high performance engine, P (*Panzer-motor*), tank engine.

Both engines were of the wet liner type and had eight bearing crankshafts. Valve gear was operated by camshafts gear driven from the flywheel.

Above:
The driver's position on an Ausf G showing the left epicyclic steering unit, both steering levers and gear change lever. *(TM)*

Far Left:
Foot controls for the driver follow the usual layout for vehicles. From left: clutch pedal, footbrake pedal and accelarator. *(TM)*

Right:
Ausf Gs fitted with roadwheels and drive sprockets await the fitting of tracks. Note the oblong-shaped opening at the front of the superstructure over which an assembly plate with the vision devices and hatches (for driver and gunner) was fitted.
In the background is a line of Jagdpanthers awaiting completion. The location is the MNH factory at Hannover in early 1945. *(TM)*

Right:
The engine bay: at the top are the oil reservoir tank (left) and the radiator's expansion tank (right). The carburettors are protected from dust by two circular multi-element air filters. *(TM)*

Below:
The left side radiator fan fitted on an Ausf G. It is the type developed for the Russian front, to supply warm air to the crew compartment. Note the delivery duct has been removed. *(TM)*

To keep pace with tank production Maybach was required to produce approximately 1,000 of these powerful V-12 engines per month and to this end had to subcontract production to Daimler-Benz, Auto-Union and other companies.

Access to the engine was via a large inspection hatch located in the centre of the rear decking. The (water) cooling system used four radiators (two on each side of the engine compartment), linked by a compensating tank. Two fans drew air through them, the hot air being expelled via grilles in the engine decking. Some heat could be directed into the turret through an air duct in order to assist the crew to keep warm in the bitter cold of the Russian winter. The engine was difficult to keep cool, especially in the summer weather, because of unit size and the lack of space in the engine compartment. A fire extinguisher system was fitted which automatically activated when the engine temperature rose over 120^{0}C (normal running temperature was 80^{0}C), spraying a special liquid from six nozzles over the fuel pump and carburettors. A warning light was fitted on the driver's instrument panel, so that the engine could be stopped and allowed to cool off. Fuel, 161 gals (731.5 litres) of petrol was carried in a total of five fuel tanks, two each side of the engine compartment and one at the rear.

Performance:

Ausf D (HL 210 P30)

RANGE:

Road:	105 miles (169km)
Cross country:	52.8 miles (85km)

FUEL CONSUMPTION:

Road:	.64mpg (.23km/l)
Cross country:	.38mpg (.13km/l)

Ausf D (late model) Ausf A and G (HL 230 P30)

RANGE:

Road:	110 miles (177km)
Cross country:	55.3 miles (89km)

FUEL CONSUMPTION:

Road:	.81mpg (.28km/l)
Cross country:	.40mpg (.14km/l)

MAXIMUM SPEED (all models):

Road:	28.6mph (46km/h)
Cross country:	14.9mph (24km/h)

Above:
The powerful V-12 Maybach engine. The HL 210 P30 versions capacity was 21,350cc (21.35ltr) and it developed 650hp at 3000rpm. The later model, HL 230 P30, had engine capacity increased to 23,880cc (23.88ltr) and developed 700hp at 3,000rpm. These 60^{0}C V-12 engines had wet liner cylinders, overhead camshafts and eight-bearing crankshafts. To keep up with demand (1,000 engines each month), Maybach licensed other companies, including Auto-Union and Daimler-Benz for production. *(TM)*

53

Right:
The Zahnradfabrik,
Friedrichshafen
(ZF) type AK7-200
gearbox fitted in all
Panthers except the
Bergepanther which
fitted the AK7-400.
Both types were all
synchromesh and had
seven forward gears
and one reverse.
In the foreground is
the engine hand-
starting handle. *(TM)*

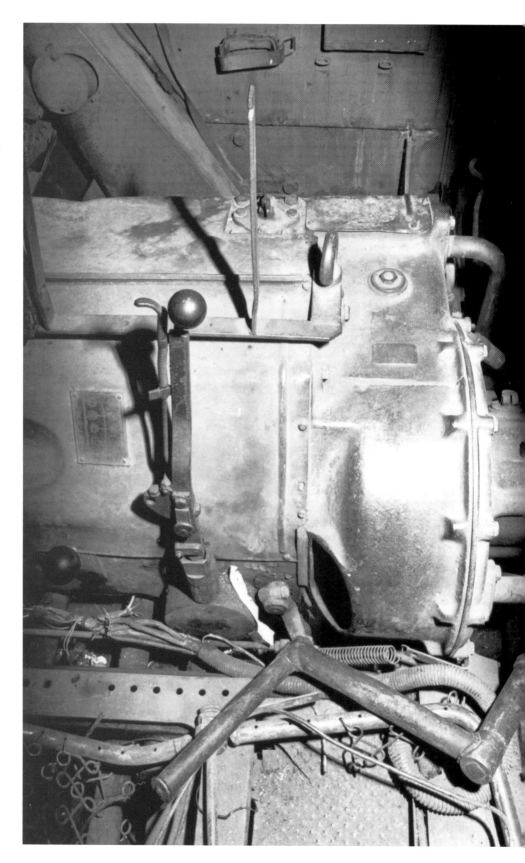

Left:
The complete gearbox mounted between the driver's and gunner/wireless operator's seats. Radio equipment was located above the gearbox. *(TM)*

Below:
The hull side in the driver's position. Note the spring loaded access hatch. *(TM)*

Right:
A knocked-out Panther Ausf G. Note the rubber tyre which has peeled off the road wheel. *(TM)*

Below right:
Spare track links were carried on special mounting racks, at the rear, on both sides of the tank. *(TM)*

Below:
Detail showing the massive cast steel towing link (two carried, one each side) and the gun barrel clamp, for when the tank was in transit. *(TM)*

Left:
Engineers testing a
Panther hull in a water
tank at the Henschel
factory. The vehicle
could ford water to
a depth of 4.60ft
(1.40m). *(TM)*

Power from the engine to the gearbox and final drive passed through an LAG3/70H dry plate clutch. On early Ausf Ds steering was by the usual Wilson-type epicycle clutch/brake system as fitted to the PzKpfw IV. This was soon replaced by new steering gear and brakes designed by MAN. Although working on the epicyclic brake/clutch system, steering was now assisted by hydraulically-operated Argus disc brakes.

The Panther's suspension was of twin torsion bar type with eight double-interleaved bogie wheels on each side. The wheels were dished with solid rubber tyres, although a few late production models were fitted with all-steel wheels (Ausf G). The first, third, fifth and seventh wheels (counting from the front) consisted of double wheels, while the second, fourth, sixth and eighth consisted of spaced wheels overlapping the others on the inside and outside. A single return roller, fitted inside between the first bogey wheel and the driving sprocket, could not be easily seen from the outside. Each set of

bogies was mounted, by means of a radius arm, to a torsion bar which was coupled in series to a second mounted in parallel. This was a new development and its effect was the same as employing a torsion bar of twice the width of the hull. The bogey wheels on the right side were set behind the torsion bar, while those on the left side lay in front. It was a complicated suspension system, difficult to maintain and heavy to work on, but it gave an excellent, smooth ride.

The two tracks were 2.15ft (65cm) wide with 86 links on the Ausf D and 2.17ft (66cm) wide with 87 links on the Ausf A and G. Tension was controlled by the rear-mounted idlers. The drive sprockets were quite high off the ground so the tank had an excellent vertical step performance, 3ft (91.44cm) as compared with 1.08ft (33cm) for PzKpfw IV and 2.58ft (79 cm) for Tiger. For really difficult terrain grousers were provided for fitting to every fifth link, in order to improve traction, but the vehicle's speed had then to be severely reduced.

CHAPTER THREE

FIGHTING COMPARTMENT

The design of the fighting compartment followed the standard German pattern – a turntable basket suspended below the turret ring by tubular supports. There were seats for the gunner and loader whilst the commander had a tip-up seat under the cupola, the same layout for all Panthers.

The turret was centrally placed on the fighting compartment and had a rotating floor. The side, front and rear walls, each made of a single piece of rolled steel armour plate, formed the main structure to which the roof and turret base were welded – the sides being sloped so that the overall width was greater than the internal diameter. The sides were constructed using two large plates, bent inwards near the rear ends to meet the edges of a comparatively narrow rear plate, so that they made the shape of a horseshoe. The roof sloped down towards the mantlet at approximately 6^0, while the sides and rear were set at 65^0 and the mantlet at 78^0. The turret skirt and front wall were welded to the turret base - a recess being machined on the underside of the ring to fit an inner ball race – thus enabling the turret to be located centrally on the hull. The turret outer ball race was bolted onto a ring riveted to the top of the hull, and was packed with grease to prevent the ingress of anything that might interrupt its smooth rotation. This method of assembly remained exactly the same throughout production of the Panther series.

The turntable, in the fighting compartment, was a large disc of aluminium 'chequer' plate riveted to a steel framework. It was slung from the turret base by four steel tubes approximately 2in (51mm) diameter - the two front tubes forming a 'V' where they joined the turntable - thus giving three point suspension. As this assembly had little lateral stiffness it was stabilized by a central iron pot, machined on the underside to a spigot which was located in rotary base junction housing welded to the floor of the hull. An opening ran from the centre to the back edge of the turntable to enable access (by traversing) to parts of the lower hull.

Three members of the crew (commander, gunner and loader) occupied the fighting compartment, with the commander on the left at the rear under the cupola, the gunner, also at the left, in front of the commander. The loader was positioned to the right of the gun.

The 7.5cm KwK 42 L/70 gun was mounted to a fabricated armour steel torsion box, with the breech block, buffer and recoil assembly. The large breech of the main armament almost divided the turret into two. The curved cast mantlet was secured to the front of the torsion box assembly. The commander's cupola was some 10.24in (26cm) high with six horizontal slots, fitted with *Ersatzgläser* blocks around the

(cont p6)

Above:
A new Ausf A being inspected by Panzerwaffe officers. Note the cover over the mantlet and the cover over the main gun. This was to hide improvements, particularly to the gun which now fitted a double-baffle muzzle brake, thus increasing muzzle velocity and killing power. *(TM)*

Left:
Turret and fighting compartment basket for the Ausf D. Note the high cupola and smoke grenade launchers. On the floor of the basket is the hydraulic power take-off unit to traverse the turret and elevate the main gun. *(GF)*

Above:
The fighting compartment basket on the Ausf G. Note the gunner's seat and the folding seat (which is under the cupola) for the commander. *(TM)*

Right:
The fighting compartment from the loader's side. Note the tubular 'A' support bracket at the front edge of the turntable base. Both illustrations are from the original Panzerwaffen Panther manuals. *(TM)*

Above:
The cupola on a late Ausf G (hatch partly open) showing the Ersatzgläser viewing blocks. These are held in place by a simple spring lock mechanism. *(TM)*

Left:
The hatch operating mechanism and lock clamp on an Ausf G. The handle was turned to raise the turret lid which, when fully raised, was swung out to the left. *(TM)*

Above:
The high-type cupola as fitted to the Panther Ausf D. Note the lid has been removed. *(TM)*

Right:
The later type cupola as fitted to the Ausf A and G models. It was machined from an homogeneous armour casting. The mountings for the episcope blocks were welded onto the casting. *(TM)*

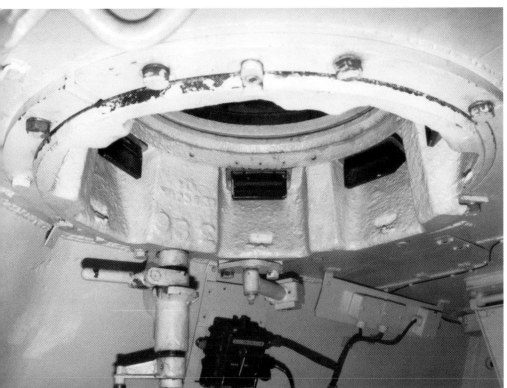

Above:
The later-type cupola showing the MG mount supported by brackets, welded to the episcope block housings. The hatch is in the open position and the operating handle (right) can be clearly seen. The cupola has received a direct hit, removing one episcope housing. *(TM)*

Left:
Inside the later-type cupola showing the episcope blocks without retaining clamps in place. *(RJF)*

Right:
The turret of an
Ausf D, showing the
small pistol port and
bung, also the large
supply hatch. Both
were deleted on the
Ausf A and G. *(TM)*

Below:
A fitter at the MNH
factory adjusts the
locking latch on the
main hatch on an
Ausf G. The turret is
coated with *Zimmerit*
anti-magnetic mine
paste. *(TM)*

Left:
Turrets, with mantlets, await completion. Note the sole *Jagdpanther* hull. The location is the MNH factory Hannover. *(TM)*

Below:
The turret fitting-out shop at MNH. The factory at Hannover was severely damaged several times by Allied bombing. *(TM)*

Right:
The turret traversing motor on an Ausf G. *(TM)*

Below:
Hand controls for the gunner. To the left is the turret traverse position indicator and is marked in 12 divisions. On some Panthers a two dial type (as used in late Panzer IVs) was fitted. *(TM)*

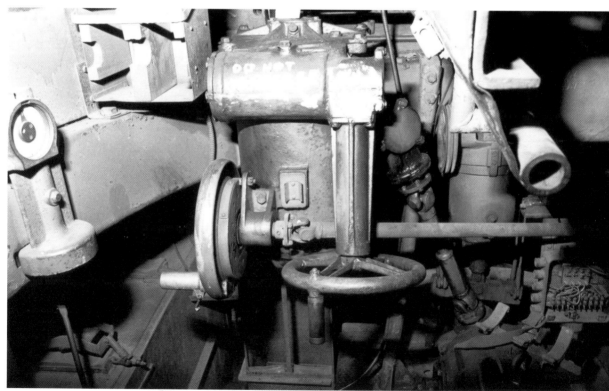

Above:
The fighting compartment. Note the recoil bars have been removed from the gun which divided the compartment. The box, at centre, is to catch spent shell cases from the breech *(TM)*

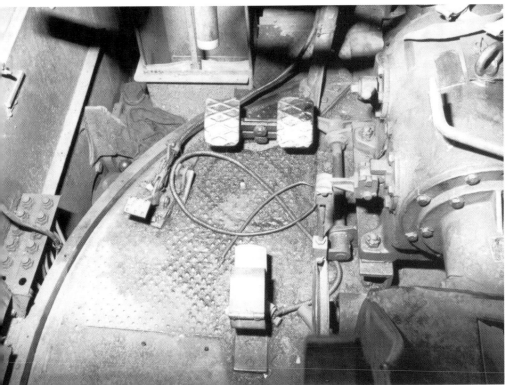

Left:
Gunner's foot controls on the turntable. Top left and right: power traverse. Left: coaxial machine gun. Bottom: main gun. *(TM)*

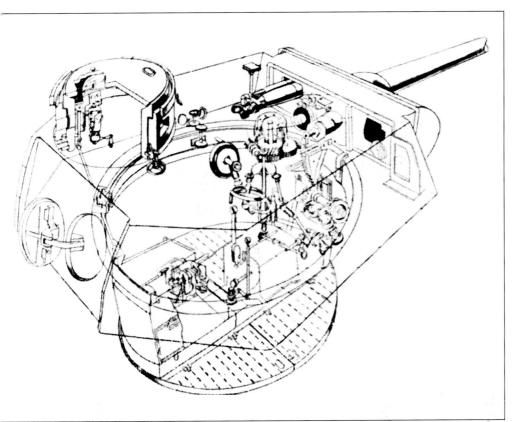

ircumference. These slots were closed by operating a handwheel inside the turret which made a 2.2in (56mm) thick steel slotted ring to rotate around the cupola. It also had a circular hatch which could be raised and then swung to one side. As has been earlier explained, this cupola was replaced on the Ausf A by a much improved, cast metal version fitted with seven armoured glass periscope ports. On the hatch ring there was a mounting for an anti-aircraft MG 34. A Panther crew always suffered from poor close-in visibility, due to the height and shape of the vehicle, although the better cupola, and later a periscope for the loader, did improve the situation.

Power for the hydraulic turret traverse was obtained from the main driveshaft via a fluid coupling, so the rate of turn depended upon engine speed, the driver and gunner working as a team to produce fast traversing. For example, in a high gear ratio, at 2,500rpm, the turret could be traversed in around 18 seconds, while in a low gear ratio at 1,000rpm it took around 03 seconds. Final target adjustments were always made by hand, so the power traverse lever on the gunner's right had to be set in the vertical (neutral) position. To traverse, this lever

was pulled back to move left and pushed forward to move right. Hand traverse was not easy, one full turn of the handwheel only moved the 7.4 tons (7,518kg) turret a mere 0.36^0.

On the Ausf D there was a bank of three smoke grenade dischargers on either side of the turret, but later a *Nahverteidigungswaffe* (close defence grenade launcher) was fitted into the turret roof, with its 92mm bore short barrel angled at approximately 60^0. This weapon had all-round traverse, was hand-operated and fired from inside the turret by a simple ring trigger. It could be used for local smoke or to fire an HE grenade.

The loader position had no access hatch until Ausf A and in the event of an emergency escape had to use the large circular replenishment port in the rear face of the turret. The pistol ports in the rear and sides were deleted on the Ausf G. For ventilation an electric fan was fitted to the right in the turret roof. There were three locks for the turret and main armament: a turret lock on the right of the turret race, an elevation lock on the gun and a barrel clamp, the latter being hinged and located on the front superstructure of the tank.

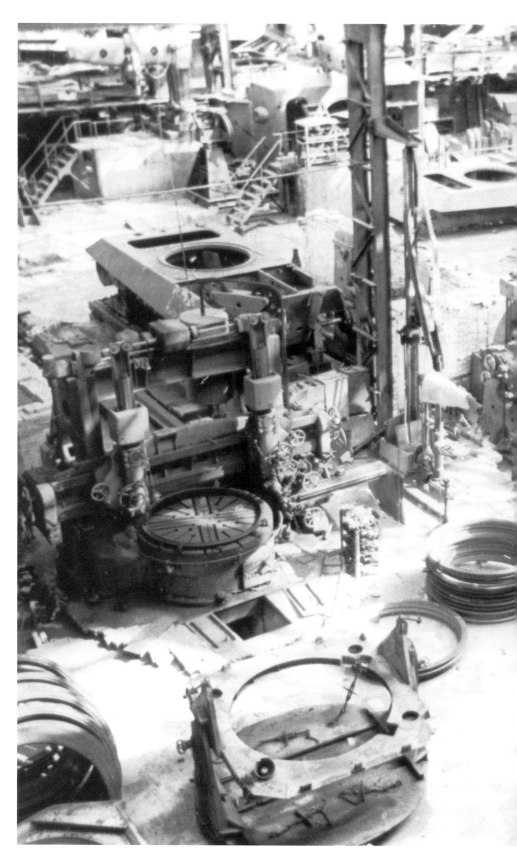

Right:
Turret traversing ball race rings awaiting machining and fitting to turrets. Note (at the left) the large jig boring machine with a turret ring in place on the turntable. *(TM)*

CHAPTER FOUR

ARMAMENT

The armament fitted to all Panthers remained the same throughout production. The only improvement to the 7.5cm KwK 42 L/70 main gun was the fitting of a double-baffle muzzle brake to increase muzzle velocity. All machine guns coaxial, hull and AA were the 7.92mm MG 34.

The Panther's main armament was the 7.5cm Kwk 42 L/70 gun, a formidable weapon, 19.19ft (5.85m) long including the muzzle brake. It was developed and manufactured by Rheinmetall Borsig, whose principal works were located at Düsseldorf-Derendorf. It could penetrate 3.55in (90mm) of armour plate at 500yd (457m) or 3.15in (80mm) at 1,000yd (915m). It could knock out a Soviet T-34 head on at 875yd (800m), or an Allied Sherman at 1,090yd (1,000m), while for side and rear engagements the official range was 3,060yd (2,800m). However, it could destroy enemy tanks at much greater ranges if the strike was in the right place - and good optical equipment along with sound training ensured a high degree of crew competency. Alongside the main armament on all Panther models there was a coaxial 7.92mm MG 34, the barrel of which did not protrude through the mantlet, with an additional glacis letterbox-type flap MG port on the Ausf D and ball-mounted 7.92mm MG 34 in the glacis on the Ausf A and G. Also on these last two models the turret pistol ports were deleted, being replaced by the *Nahverteidigungswaffe* (close-in defence weapon) - a short-barrelled grenade projector,

operated from within the turret, for firing *Nebelkerzen* (smoke grenades) or high explosive (HE) grenades. In addition there was a exterior ring fitted on the cupola of both models to mount another MG 34.

All German World War Two tank main gun shared similar features: electric primer firing hydraulic and hydro-pneumatic recoil gea and a Hotchkiss-type semi-automatic spring operated, vertical sliding, breech block operation. The main gun was mounted in fabricated torsion box assembly, which also ha apertures for the gunsight and coaxial MG mounting. On each side of the box a moving trunnion was fitted to this assembly which allowed up and down movement of the gun with the complete assembly protected by th cast mantlet. The front plate casting for th turret was internally machined to provide fixed trunnion mounting at each side so tha the gun/mantlet assembly could be fitted an retained by mounting bolts. Recoil loads wer absorbed from the buffer and recuperato cylinders by the torsion box. The gunner an loader were protected from breech recoil an the gun's mechanism by a fabricated tubula steel cradle.

Above:
The breech and mounting assembly for the main gun. This mounting is a fabricated armour steel plate torsion box with apertures for gunsight and coaxial machine gun. At each side is a moving trunnion block for mounting the assembly into the fixed trunnions machined in the turret front plate casting. *(TM)*

Left:
The double-muzzle brake as fitted to the 7.5cm KwK 42 L/70 gun on later Panthers. *(TM)*

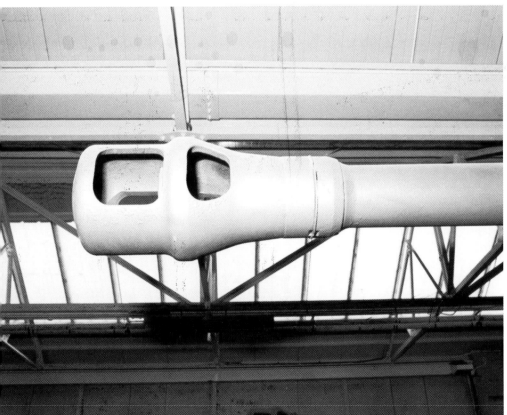

Right:
The Hotchkiss-type breech block in the ready to load position. To the right is the mounting for the MG 34 coaxial machine gun. The recoil protection bars have been removed from the breech. Note the ducting to the roof-mounted ventilation fan. *(TM)*

The breech mechanism was of the French-designed Hotchkiss type. A breech ring was secured to the gun barrel by a retaining ring and a breech block slid vertically in the breech ring, operated by an internal crank, keyed to the breech mechanism lever situated on the right side of the breech ring.

The gun itself was fired by an electric firing pin which projected through the face of the breech block and made contact with the cartridge primer. This pin would have to be withdrawn before the breech could be opened, so a safety catch was installed that could lock both the entire mechanism and/or the firing pin.

A pair of claw-shaped extractors were mounted on a transverse shaft just forward of the breech block, to withdraw the spent cartridge when the the breech was opened. Hooks on the claw's backs caught the block when lowered - and held it open until released by the insertion of a new round or else by pressing the extractor release lever.

The gunner's main controls were all power operated, except for fine handwheel adjustments, from pedals mounted on the turntable floor. If power failed the turret could be operated manually. The coax MG could be fired by floor pedal or conventional trigger. The main gun was sighted by a Leitz TZF 12 binocular-type telescope on the Ausf D (later a TZF 12a monocular on the Ausf A and G) marked with range scales for all types of ammunition carried - the HE scale also being used for aiming the machine gun. It gave dual magnification and included a range plate and a sighting plate. The range plate had the scale for main armament and co-axial MG ranges marked around the edge. It rotated about its own axis, while the sighting plate, which contained sighting and aim-off markings, moved up and down. Both plates turned together. Thus, to obtain a selected range, the gunner turned the range wheel until the correct marking was opposite a pointer on top of the sight, then laid the sighting mark on the target by using his traverse and elevating handwheels. German gun sights consisted of a circle of Vs, pointing inwards towards the centre, which remained clear, rather than the more familiar crossed hair sights. This allowed for even greater accuracy as there was nothing in the centre of the sight to detract from the target silhouette.

Gun position in relation to the tank was

(cont p80)

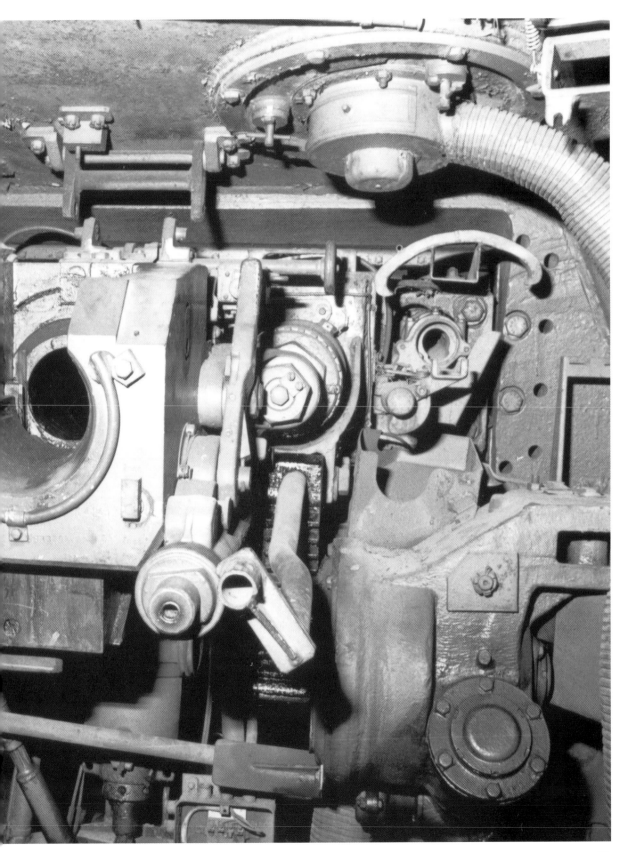

Right:
The cast armour turret front plate on an Ausf D. *(TM)*

Right:
A fixed trunnion mounting was machined into each side of the cast front plate. The gun and torsion box assembly was located in the trunnions and held in place by a series of heavy bolts. *(TM)*

Right:
The cast armour mantlet fitted over the barrel and protected the main gun torsion box assembly. *(TM)*

Left:
The wireless operator/hull gunner's position with the MG 34 and mounting in position. Note to the right, the gunner's 2 o'clock position, is the episcope vision device. *(RJF)*

Below:
The ball-mounting for the hull MG 34. The smaller hole is for the gunsight. *(RJF)*

Another view of the turret assembly shop at the MNH works in Hannover. The turrets are for Panther Ausf G and the guns are 7.5cm KwK 42 L/70 with double-baffled muzzle brakes. *(TM)*

shown via a two-dial indicator for the gunner (the left dial having an inner scale marked 0-12 and an outer scale 0-64, for coarse adjustment, while the right-hand dial was graduated in millimetres for fine adjustment). There was also a 1-12 clock scale marked on a toothed ring around the inside of the commander's cupola. The cupola scale worked on the contra-rotation principle, so that when the turret was traversed a pinion, whic[h] engaged with the teeth of the turret rack, dro[ve] the scale in the opposite direction but [at] the same speed. This meant that the figu[re] 12 on the scale always remained pointin[g] directly ahead along the vehicle centre lin[e]. The commander used this to estimate th[e] approximate bearing to the next target. Th[e] indicator was used less when the later cupo[la]

Above:
The Panzer Museum's
superbly restored
PzKpfw V Ausf A
Befehlswagen
(Command Tank). *(RJF)*

Above:
The Panzer Museum's
superbly restored
PzKpfw V Ausf A
Befehlswagen
(Command Tank). *(RJF)*

Left:
The same tank in
action. Note the
distinctive aerials
as fitted to the
Command Tank. *(RJF)*

was fitted because the commander then had to be in the 'head down' position in order to use vision ports, and also had a clear view of the gunner's traverse indicator.

A total of 79 main armament rounds were carried on Ausf A and D (increased to 82 for Ausf G), stowed in racks and lockers within the lower half of the fighting compartment; 4,500 rounds of MG 34 ammunition were carried.

The main gun used the standard fixed QF (Quick Fire) ammunition and fired four types of shell: HE (High Explosive) and APCBC (Armour Piercing , Capped, Ballistic Capped), AP (Armoured Piercing) and smoke. In most cases composite-rigid, tungsten carbide cored projectiles were provided until Germany's supply of the metallic element tungsten was exhausted.

CHAPTER FIVE

MARKINGS & INSIGNIA

The Panther first entered battlefront service at
Kursk in Operation *Zitadelle*. The vehicles carried the
Balkenkreuz on the front superstructure above the
main drive sprocket and at the rear. They were also
numbered using standard *Panzerwaffe* stencilling

The Panther, being a heavy cruiser tank, was intended to have been the main armament of the German Armoured Division. Later a war department directive appeared equipping each Panzer Regiment almost entirely with the type, together with a number of Tiger heavy tanks. Inevitably this was altered due to a restriction in production of both types as the war drew to a close. The Tiger was then relegated to a heavy company and each regiment equipped with one battalion of PzKpfw IVs and one battalion of Panthers.

The Panther was first issued to 51st and 52nd *Panzerabteilungen* (Panzer Battalions) and first saw action at Kursk in Russia, 4 July 1943. Most of the Ausf D production went to these units, also to the 23rd and 26th Independent Panzer Regiments, as well as the Das Reich and Leibstandarte Adolf Hitler SS Panzer Divisions. Later other units equipped with the Panther included 1st, 2nd and 12th Hitlerjugend SS Panzer Regiments and 130th Panzer Lehr Regiment as well as 2nd and 9th Panzer Divisions. By October 1943 there were four more Panzer Divisions in the Waffen-SS: 3rd Totenkopf, 5th Wiking, 9th Hohenstaufen and 10th Frundsberg. Primarily, the Panther's

homeground was on the eastern front, bu[t] numbers were seen in the western (Normand[y] and Ardennes) and southern European (Italy[)] theatres, as well as in the final defence o[f] Germany.

As regards to identification and concealmen[t] although the Germans liked regularity an[d] would have preferred a standard format fo[r] all their vehicles, they were forced to adapt t[o] the circumstances of geography, supply an[d] combat, eventually learning the benefits an[d] the necessity of both battlefield identificatio[n] and camouflage.

Basically, as a rule of thumb, there were fou[r] types of signage: national, divisional, tactica[l] and personal. (A fifth perhaps is the vehicl[e] chassis production number.)

Balkenkreuz

The *Balkenkreuz* (Balkan Cross) was th[e] national symbol eventually carried by almos[t] every German World War Two military vehicl[e] although there was considerable variation an[d] modification. After the early Polish campaig[n]

(cont p9[*)*]

Above:
The Panther was first deployed in Operation *Zitadelle* (Citadel), the attack on Kursk in 1943. Due to engine fires, and gearbox/transmission and track failures only a few reached the battlefront. *(TM)*

Left:
A rear view of a Ausf G. Note the left side exhaust mounting has been modified to carry three pipes in an attempt to alleviate a problem in which the single pipe glowed red at night. The three pipes were intended to improve exhaust gas flow. *(TM)*

Panzer-Gruppen/Panzer-Armeen

Panzer-Gruppe 1/1
Panzer-Armee

Panzer-Gruppe 2/2
Panzer-Armee

Panzer-Gruppe 3/3
Panzer-Armee

Panzer-Gruppe 4/4
Panzer-Armee

5 Panzer-Armee

Armee-Korps (mot.)/Panzerkorps

III. Panzerkorps

IV. Panzerkorps

XXIV. Panzerkorps

XXXXVI. Panzerkorps

XXXXVII. Panzerkorps

XXXXVIII. Panzerkorps

Panzer Division signs, 1943-1945

1st Panzer Division

2nd Panzer Division

3rd Panzer Division

4th Panzer Division

5th Panzer Division

6th Panzer Division

7th Panzer Division

8th Panzer Division

9th Panzer Division

11th Panzer Division

13th Panzer Division

14th Panzer Division

16th Panzer Division

19th Panzer Division

20th Panzer Division

21st Panzer Division

23rd Panzer Division

26th Panzer Division

116th Panzer Division

Panzer-Lehr-Division

Right:
A troop of *Panzer-grenadiers* pass by a Panther Ausf A during action on the Russian front. The soldier in the foreground carries a *Spandau* machine gun whilst behind him another carries a *Panzerfaust* anti-tank grenade launcher. At the rear of the Panther (standing on the decking) are three high rank German officers. *(TM)*

Panzer Regiment signs, 1943-1945

2nd Panzer Regiment

3rd Panzer Regiment

4th Panzer Regiment

1st Abt. 4th Panzer Regiment

6th Panzer Regiment

11th Panzer Regiment

23rd Panzer Regiment

26th Panzer Regiment

31st Panzer Regiment

33rd Panzer Regiment

1st Abt. 33rd Panzer Regiment

35th Panzer Regiment

Panzer-Lehr-Regiment 130

I./Panzer-Lehr-Regiment 130

II./Panzer-Lehr-Regiment 130

201st Panzer Regiment
Regimental Staff

201st Panzer Regiment
1 Abteilung

201st Panzer Regiment
2 Abteilung

201st Panzer Regiment
3 Abteilung

Panzer-Abteilungen signs, 1943-1945

Left: 2 variants,
Panzer-Abteilung 51
Allocated to Panzer-Grenadier
Division "Kurmark",
February 1945

Schwere
Panzer-Abteilung 501

Panzer-Abteilung C

Panzer-Abteilung
"Schlesien"

National Insignia 1942-1945

1940-1942, Standard

1940-1945, Variant

1943-1945, Variant

1940-1945, Variant

**Turret
Numbers**

Above:
An Ausf A being examined by Allied troops in Italy. The tank appears to be intact, having been knocked-out by a single shot into the side of the turret. Note the white identification patches painted around the top edge of the turret. *(TM)*

the lessons learned led to the development of the stencilled silhouette *Balkenkreuz*, which, with the expansion of conflict to multiple fronts, had its own four main regional variants. These consisted of a white silhouette cross-edged in black to various degrees, the centre either reflecting the vehicle's original colour or overpainted with another - usually either black or white and the ends of the cross being usually left open. It was basically similar in proportion to that of the cross in the centre of the *Luftwaffe* insignia, being essentially a silhouette of the original solid cross. In Europe initially most AFVs were *Wehrmacht* grey and the white *Balkenkreuz* black-centred and black-outlined. In Russia vehicles were snow camouflaged in winter with varying degrees of professionalism according to time and supply of materials. Here the *Balkenkreuz* could be outlined in black, completely black or painted in white onto a black field. Later, still, in Europe as the Allies closed in there was a bewildering array of paints/camouflage used and usually one of the four main *Balkenkreuz* variants.

The state of air cover also influenced circumstances. When there was a danger of friendly fire the engine decks were often draped with the *Nazi* flag - black *Swastika* in

a white circle on a red background. Also broa white recognition bands or rectangles wer used. All soon vanished after air supremac was lost.

All divisions and regiments had the own emblem, whether or not it was displaye on the battlefield. They were used to identif vehicles but were also an important facto in the bonding of each particular unit. The later took the form of individual pictori designs, often (like the later tank names) of larg predators, but encompassing a wide spectrur of other elements including heraldry, loc provinces of origin and specific campaign However, up until 1941 the actual battlefie divisional signs were closely monitored by th German High Command, and there was a ru that Panzer Divisions should carry simp geometrical designs or runic symbols as the combat identification. Their success w, confirmed in the Polish campaign where the helped deny the enemy knowledge of th formations encountered. Their official designated colour was yellow but whi eventually became more usual.

Despite the later additional division pictorial emblems this geometric/run marking system remained the essenti

Above:
At the end of World War Two enough Panthers were abandoned in France to allow the French to equip almost two battalions. The Panther shown has the Free French Army badge on the turret side and is displayed in Paris in the late 1950s. *(TM)*

Panzer Tactical Signs 1942-1945

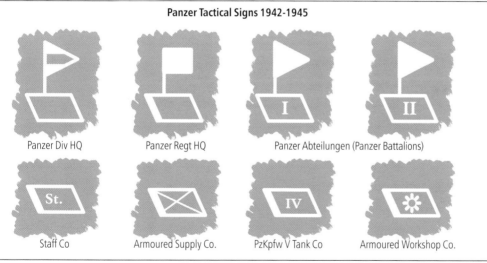

Panzer Div HQ

Panzer Regt HQ

Panzer Abteilungen (Panzer Battalions)

St.

Staff Co

Armoured Supply Co.

IV

PzKpfw V Tank Co

Armoured Workshop Co.

attlefield divisional sign.

By the time of the Panther's introduction, actical information for German AFVs was onveyed by large white and red stencilled ettering on the side or rear of the turret. These large red turret numbers were normally dged in white but the red centres were ventually replaced with black, which remained he prominent colour until the close of the var, although (just to confuse things) they were sometimes completely white or white-edged in black. A final version did see the numbers outlined in either red, black or white with the original base colour of the vehicle showing through. These number systems almost always had three digits. The last digit on the right stood for the tank's position within the troop; the middle number for the position of that troop within the company and the first digit on the left was the company number.

Panzer Divisions - Waffen SS.

1943-45   Kursk   1942-45   Kursk

   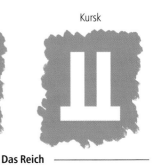

————— **Leibstandarte SS Adolf Hitler** —————   ————— **Das Reich** —————

1942-45   Kursk   Kursk

————————— **Totenkopf** —————————

1943-44   1944-45   1944   1944

————— **Wiking** —————   ————— **Hohenstaufen** —————

1942-45   Kursk   Kursk   1944

————— **Frundsberg** —————   ————— **Hitlerjugend** —————

Panzer Grenadier Divisions

Grossdeutschland

3rd Panzer Regiment

4th Panzer Regiment

Brandenburg

Kumark

25th Panzer Grenadier Div.

20th Panzer Grenadier Div.

20th Panzer Grenadier Div.

Hermann Göring Division and Panzerkorps

Division HQ

9th Panzer Regiment

HQ 2nd Panzer Regiment

As well as these regular numbers certain vehicles carried letters as a variation or addition signifying other roles and seniority. There were also those that bore the Roman numerals I or II, usually as a prefix, denoting command vehicles.

There was always a small percentage of individual personal signage. However, after 1942, with the war having expanded onto various fronts, the choice and application of signs depended increasingly on more junior commanders and there emerged a degree of more overt personal signage. These included individual elements such as animals, playing cards and girls names for their resonances and associations. By 1944 things had become still more confused as the *Panzerwaffe* began to disintegrate. Sometimes legitimate signs were deliberately changed to confuse enemy intelligence, as in the final German offensive in the Ardennes. There were also victory markings: barrel rings and turret kill silhouettes, often haphazardly handpainted rather than stencilled. Barrels and hulls could sport teeth and turrets faces or memorial plaques to dead crew members. *Zimmerit* anti-mine paste with its uneven surface also made neat marking more problematic.

Above:
A captured Ausf A which was used in anti-tank gunnery trials at the Longcross range in Surrey, England. *(TM)*

Far left:
The Panther head emblem painted on the turret sides of a captured vehicle displayed in Moscow, 1945. *(TM)*

Above: End of the battle – a Panther immobilised in a French village. *(TM)*